HOW TO DRAW MONSTERS

HOW TO DRAW

FRANKENSTEIN

Derrick Richards

Enslow PUBLISHING

Please visit our website, www.enslow.com. For a free color catalog of all our high-quality books, call toll free 1-800-398-2504 or fax 1-877-980-4454

Published in 2027 by
Enslow Publishing
2544 Clinton Street
Buffalo, NY 14224

Portions of this work were originally authored by Greg Roza and published as *Drawing Movie Monsters Step-by-Step: Drawing Frankenstein*. All new material in this edition is authored by Derrick Richards.

Cataloging-in-Publication Data
Names: Richards, Derrick.
Title: How to draw Frankenstein / Derrick Richards.
Description: Buffalo, NY : Enslow Publishing, 2027. | Series: How to draw monsters | Includes glossary and index.
Identifiers: ISBN 9781978548756 (pbk.) | ISBN 9781978548763 (library bound) | ISBN 9781978548770 (ebook)
Subjects: LCSH: Frankenstein's Monster (Fictitious character)--Juvenile literature. | Monsters in art--Juvenile literature. | Drawing--Technique--Juvenile literature.
Classification: LCC NC825.M6 R534 2027 | DDC 743.87--dc23

Printed in China

Photos Credits: Cover, p. 1 Shutterstock AI/Shutterstock.com; cover, p. 1, 5, 7, 9, 11, 13, 15, 17, 19, 21 (notebook) Liena10/Shutterstock.com; p. 5 (ruler) karen roach/Shutterstock.com; p. 5 (colored pencils) Avocado_studio/Shutterstock.com; p. 5 (marker) New Africa/Shutterstock.com; p. 6, 10, 16 Wikipedia/Wikipedia; p. 8, 20, 22 Shutterstock AI Generator/Shutterstock.com; p. 12 fotografiko eugen/Shutterstock.com; p.14 Summit Art Creations/Shutterstock.com; p. 18 John Kobal Foundation;

CPSIA compliance information: Batch #QSENS27: For further information, contact Enslow Publishing, New York, New York, at 1-800-398-2504.

CONTENTS

A FAMOUS MONSTER

A monster's lifeless body is strapped to a table. The **evil** scientist Dr. Frankenstein throws a switch. The dark lab fills with the buzz of machines. "It's alive!" the mad doctor shouts as his monster rises from the table.

The story of *Frankenstein* was written by Mary Shelley in 1818. It tells the tale of a young scientist who wants to create life. But when he finally succeeds, there are some terrible consequences!

In the 200 years since Shelley's novel was published, Frankenstein has become one of the most memorable movie monsters of all time. Let's learn to draw this famous monster in a few easy steps!

You will need the following supplies:

PAPER

RULER

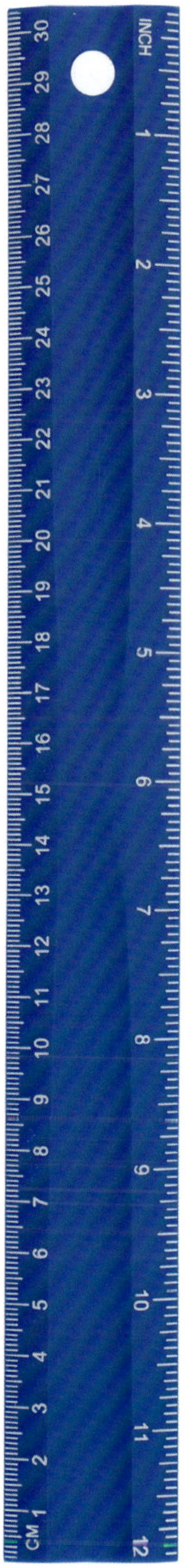

PENCIL

MARKER

COLORED PENCILS

FRANKENSTEIN'S BEGINNINGS

Though Mary Shelley's novel was written in 1818, Frankenstein didn't appear in movies until more than 100 years later. Frankenstein first appeared on the big screen in 1931 with the American movie *Frankenstein*. British actor Boris Karloff played the monster. The role made him—and Frankenstein himself—very famous!

One of the most famous lines from all monster movies is "It's alive!" Let's start by drawing Frankenstein as he first gets up from the scientist's table.

When people use the name "Frankenstein," they usually mean the monster itself. However, Frankenstein is actually the last name of the scientist who created the monster. This book uses the name Frankenstein to talk about the monster.

Step 1

Draw shapes as shown for the head and body.

Step 2

Add ovals around the body outline.

Step 3

Join the ovals with curved lines to form the arms, legs, hands, and feet.

Step 4

Add lines to make the neck, jacket, fingers, and shoes. Draw the outline of the table.

Step 5

Add details to the face, clothes, table, and lab equipment. Erase the ovals.

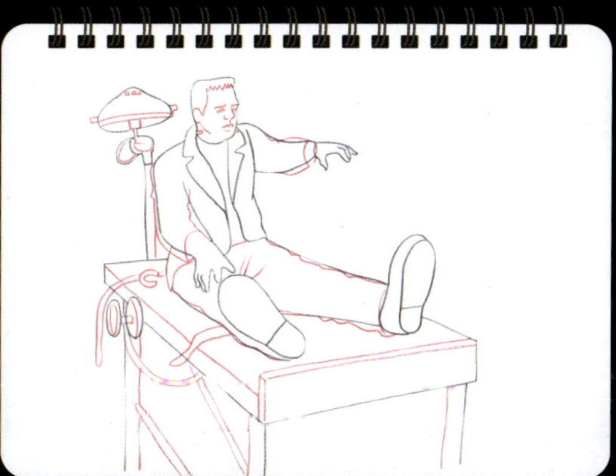

Step 6

Add details as shown. Erase extra lines.

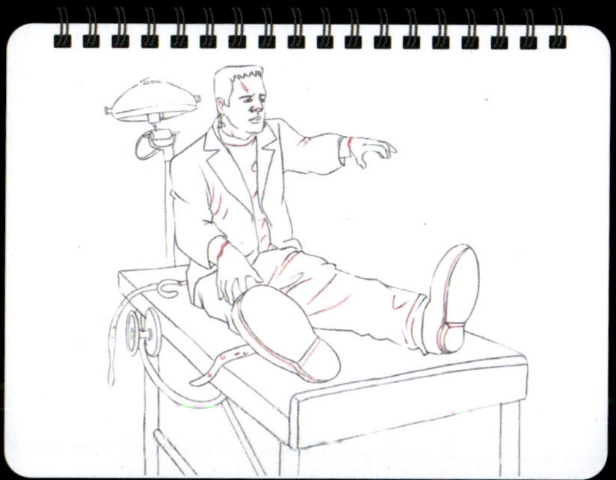

BOOK VS. MOVIE

Like most movie **adaptations**, the 1931 movie differs from the book in a handful of ways. In the novel, Dr. Frankenstein builds and brings to life a human being using materials in his lab. But in the movie, Dr. Frankenstein creates his monster from body parts that have been stolen from graves.

In the novel, the monster is angry because he is treated badly by others. In the 1931 movie, the monster is angry because the doctor gave him a criminal's brain. Either way, Frankenstein is angry! Let's draw the monster as he storms out of the laboratory.

Frankenstein is often shown as a tall, stitched-together monster who walks slowly and steadily. He is easy to recognize!

Step 1
Draw the outline of the head and a rounded rectangle for the body.

Step 2
Add small ovals as shown to guide you as you draw the arms and legs.

Step 3
Join the ovals to form the arms, legs, hands, and feet.

Step 4
Add Frankenstein's hairline, ears, jacket, fingers, and shoes. Draw the bolts on his neck.

Step 5
Add the facial features. Add detail to the clothing. Erase the guides.

Step 6
Add more details. Erase extra lines.

BECOMING FRANKENSTEIN

Actor Boris Karloff made Frankenstein famous. He played the monster in such a way that audiences were scared of him but felt sorry for him at the same time. Karloff came up with the slow Frankenstein walk. Each of Karloff's boots weighed 13 pounds (6 kg), so that might have had something to do with it!

The Frankenstein that monster-movie fans know and love has a square forehead and green skin. He also has two bolts on his neck and a scar across his forehead. Grab your pencils and try drawing a close-up of the monster's face.

Boris Karloff had to wear a lot of heavy makeup while filming. It took hours to put on each day!

Step 1
Draw the outline of the head.

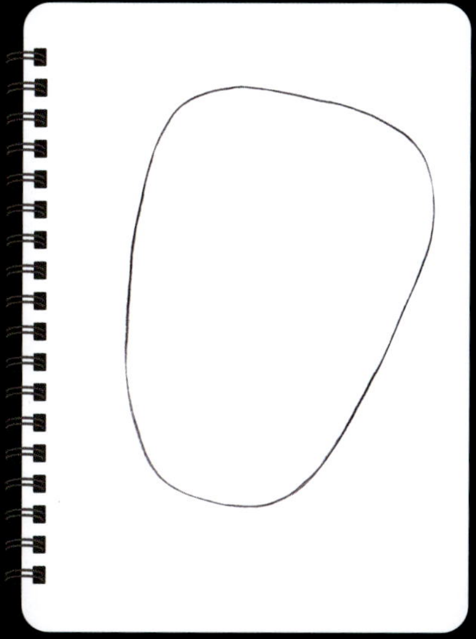

Step 2
Add the outlines of the eyes and the mouth.

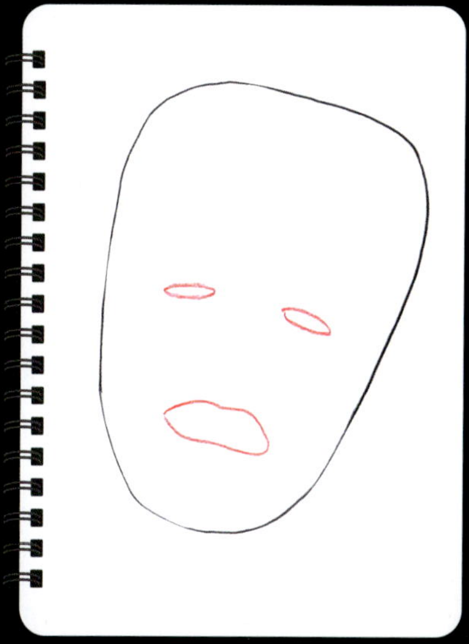

Step 3
Add the outlines of the eyebrows, ears, nose, and neck.

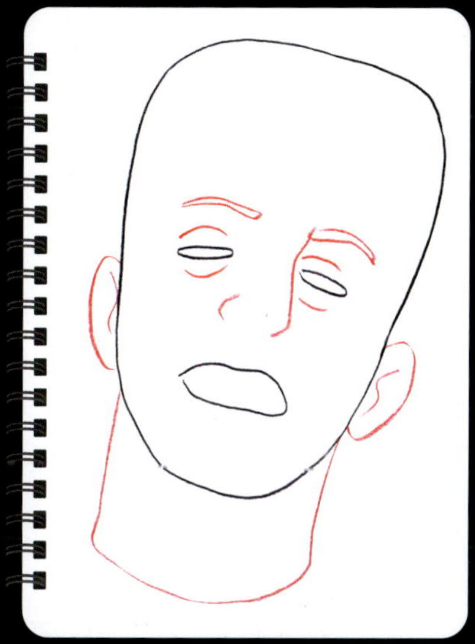

Step 4
Add Frankenstein's hairline and the outline of the lower lip.

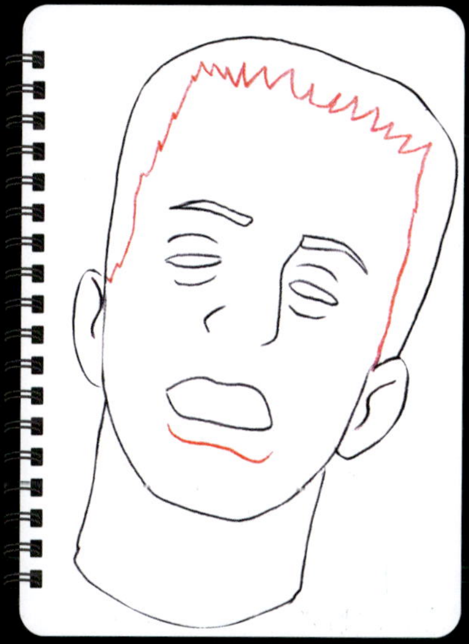

Step 5
Draw the nostrils. Add the bolts on the neck. Add details to the neck, face, and forehead.

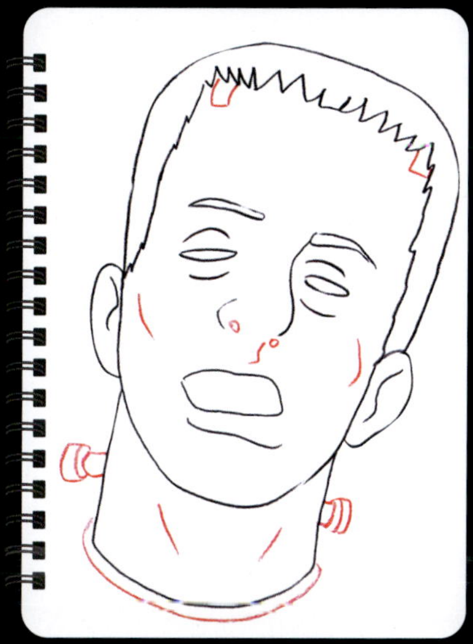

Step 6
Draw scars and lines on the face. Add shading and details to the facial features. Add shading and color.

THE MONSTER CONTINUES

Since 1931, many more movies have been made about Frankenstein. In 1935, *The Bride of Frankenstein* introduced fans to a female monster. Boris Karloff returned as Frankenstein, and Elsa Lanchester played his bride. Some say this **sequel** was even better than the first!

In 1939, Karloff played the monster once again in *The Son of Frankenstein*. In this film, Dr. Frankenstein's son tries to continue his father's work to **restore** his father's **reputation** as a scientist. But because this is a horror movie, his plan doesn't exactly work out!

In a scene from *The Bride of Frankenstein*, Frankenstein is all chained up. Let's draw it.

Most recently, Frankenstein appeared on the big screen in 2025's *Frankenstein*.

Step 1
Draw the outline of the head. Add a shape for the body.

Step 2
Add ovals to use as guides for drawing the arms and legs.

Step 3
Draw arms, legs, hands, and feet using the guides. Add lines for the neck and bolts.

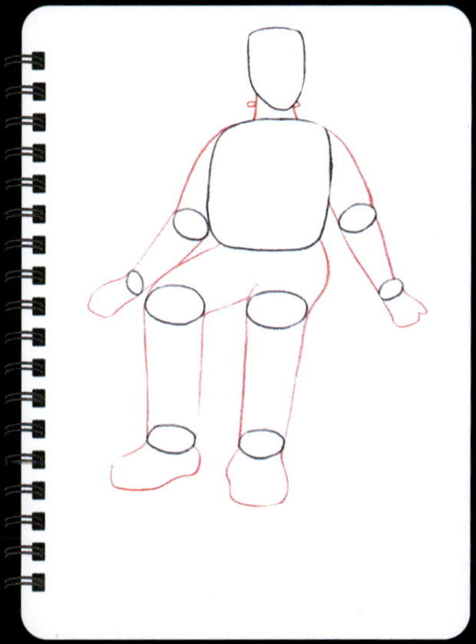

Step 4
Add the hairline, ears, and fingers. Draw the outlines of the chair and clothes. Begin the rings that hold the chains.

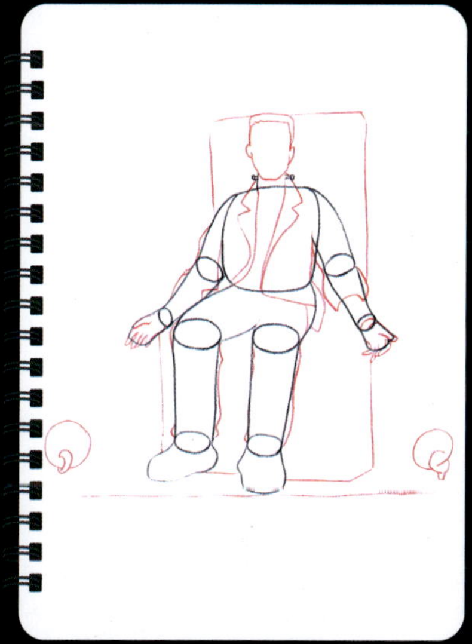

Step 5
Add the facial features and details to the chains, clothes, and chair. Erase the guides.

Step 6
Finish the drawing by adding more details.

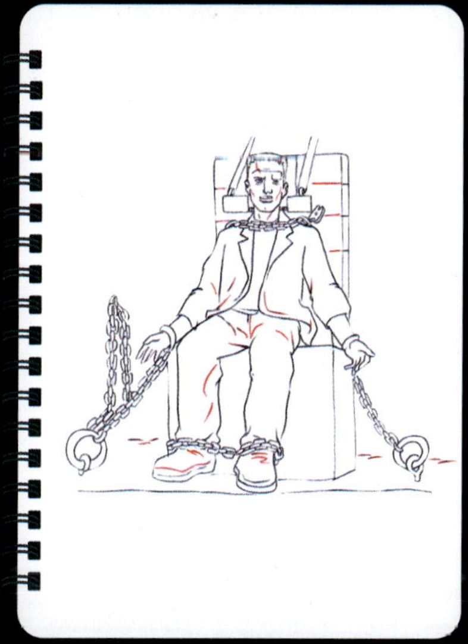

MONSTER BATTLES

Frankenstein has become one of the most popular movie **icons** of all time. He helped make other American movie monsters popular, too!

The monsters were so popular that they began appearing together in movies. Frankenstein battled the Wolf Man in the 1943 movie *Frankenstein Meets the Wolf Man*. Actor Bela Lugosi played Frankenstein in this movie. But Lugosi is most well-known for playing another movie monster, Dracula! The 1944 movie *House of Frankenstein* featured all three monsters together.

Now, let's draw Frankenstein doing his slow and unsteady walk. His hands are outstretched for balance!

Classic movie monsters such as Frankenstein, Dracula, and the Wolf Man are still popular today. Fans love to be scared!

Step 1

Draw the outlines of the head and body.

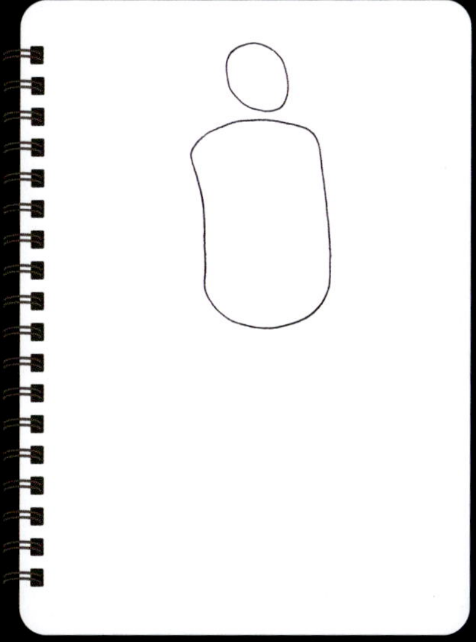

Step 2

Add round guide shapes as shown.

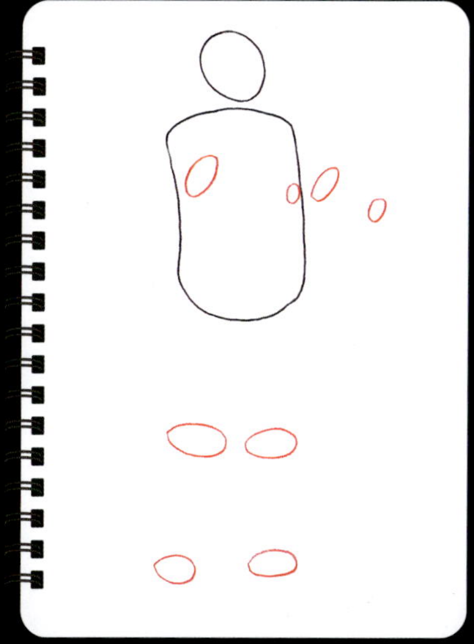

Step 3

Add lines to form the neck. Connect the guide shapes to draw the arms, hands, legs, and feet.

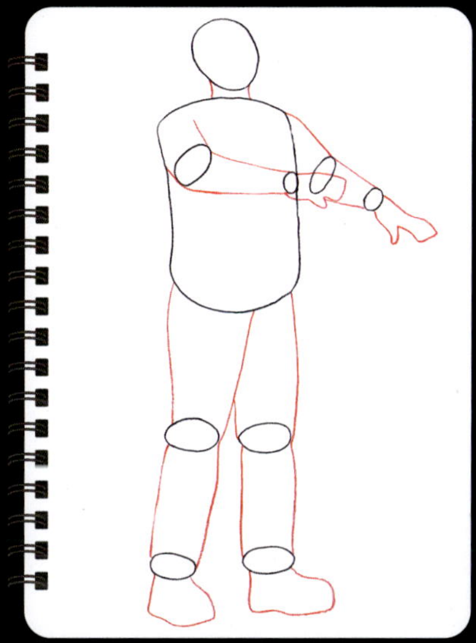

Step 4

Draw the outline of Frankenstein's face. Draw the outline of the jacket.

Step 5

Add details to the face and the clothes. Don't forget to add the bolts in Frankenstein's neck!

Step 6

Add color to your drawing.

FRANKENSTEIN EVOLVES

The American Frankenstein movies were very successful. Years later, a British film company started a new series of monster movies. These films were much more **violent** and bloody than earlier Frankenstein movies.

The 1957 British film *The* **Curse** *of Frankenstein* marked one of the first big changes to Frankenstein's famous look. This British **version** was scarier. His head was no longer square and the bolts from his neck were gone, but he had more scars and injuries to his face.

Now, let's draw the evil scientist Dr. Frankenstein as he works in his lab. But watch out! The monster is sneaking up on him.

Frankenstein isn't always scary. Sometimes he's funny and even cute, like in the 2012 film *Hotel Transylvania.*

Step 1

Start by drawing a shape for the head and a shape for the body.

Step 2

Add small, round shapes as shown.

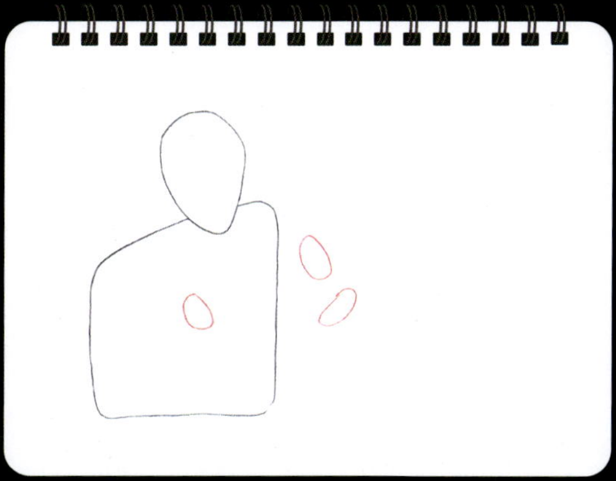

Step 3

Join the round shapes to create arms and hands. Add a line for the neck.

Step 4

Draw the outlines of the face and hands. Add the outlines of the test tube and the beaker.

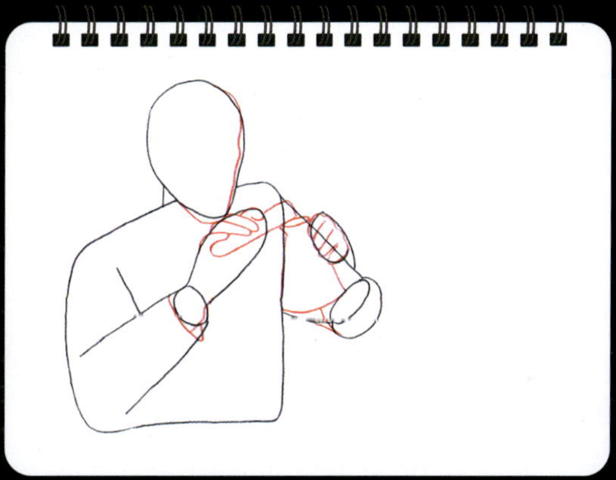

Step 5

Add the face and hair. Add detail to the clothes. Add lab equipment. Draw the outline of the monster's shadow. Erase the guides.

Step 6

Add details to Dr. Frankenstein's face, clothes, and lab equipment.

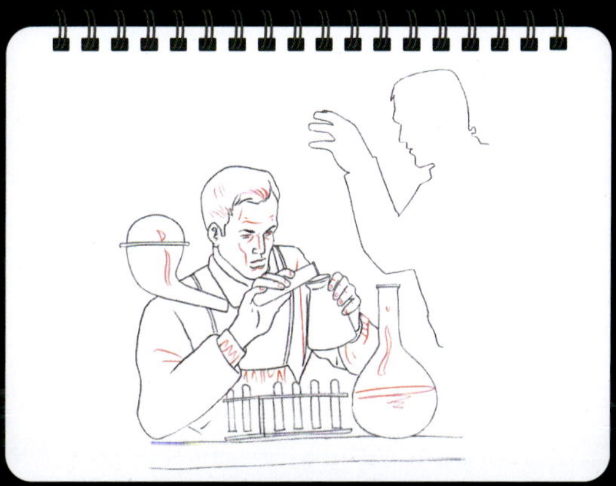

LOTS OF FRANKENSTEINS

The very first Frankenstein film was made in 1910. It is a silent film that is just 12 minutes long. Since then, more than 150 movies have been **inspired** by Mary Shelley's original novel!

In the past century, filmmakers have given fans many different versions of Frankenstein monsters to enjoy. Many Frankenstein movies are scary. Some, like the 1974 movie *Young Frankenstein*, are funny. In some movies the monster can talk. In others he just growls!

Now, let's draw Frankenstein and his bride in this scene from *Bride of Frankenstein*.

The bride of Frankenstein returned to the big screen in 2026's *The Bride*!

Step 1

Draw the shapes that will guide you in drawing the happy couple.

Step 2

Add round shapes around both bodies.

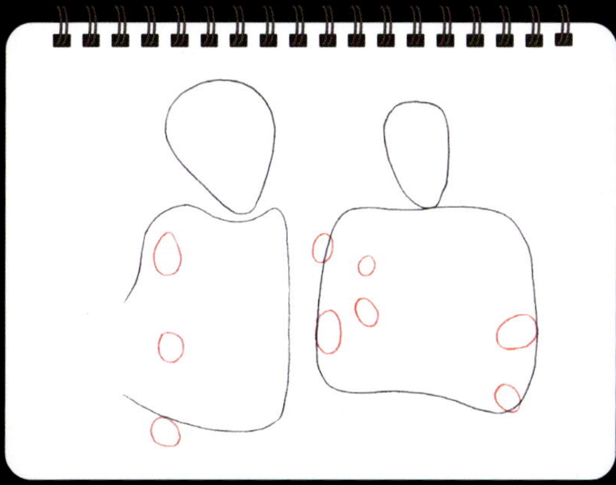

Step 3

Draw lines for the necks. Use the round shapes to draw arms and hands.

Step 4

Begin the faces and the clothes.

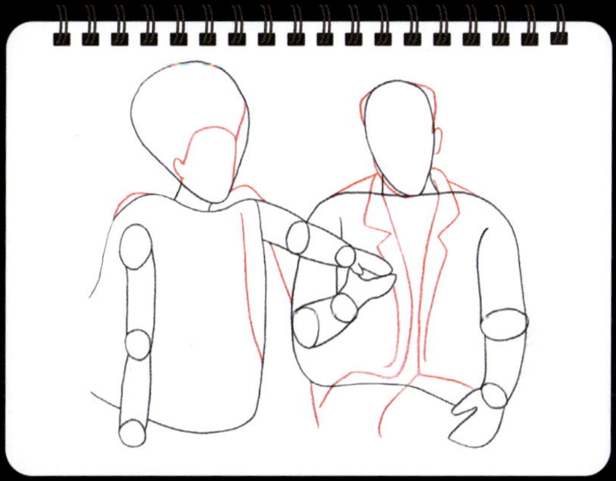

Step 5

Draw the outlines of the facial features. Add lines to show the folds in their clothing. Erase the guide shapes.

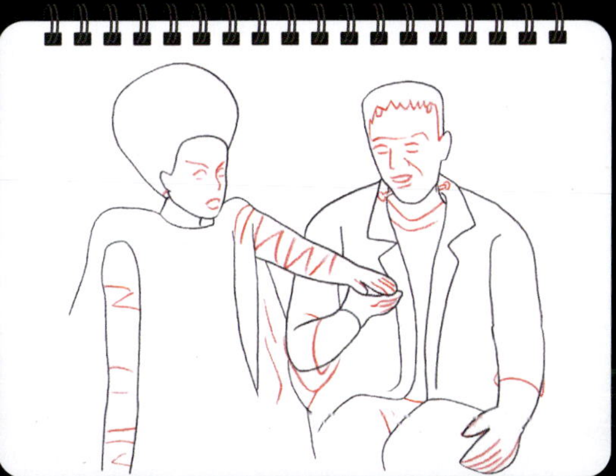

Step 6

Add details to the hair, clothes, and faces of both monsters.

A MONSTER ICON

Mary Shelley's 1818 novel led to Frankenstein as a cultural icon. Today, Frankenstein is still one of the most popular movie monsters of all time. He has appeared in hundreds of movies, short films, and TV episodes. You can find his likeness in comics, cartoons, video games, toys, and even on cereal boxes! The breakfast cereal Franken Berry showed a pink version of Frankenstein on the box.

Learning to draw Frankenstein is a great way to practice your drawing skills. And who knows, you might inspire the next great Frankenstein movie! Let's draw Frankenstein one last time.

Frankenstein himself has appeared in more than 100 movies. The character has inspired hundreds of others, too.

Step 1

Draw the outline of the head. Add a larger shape with curved edges for the outline of the body.

Step 2

Draw small circles and ovals around the body.

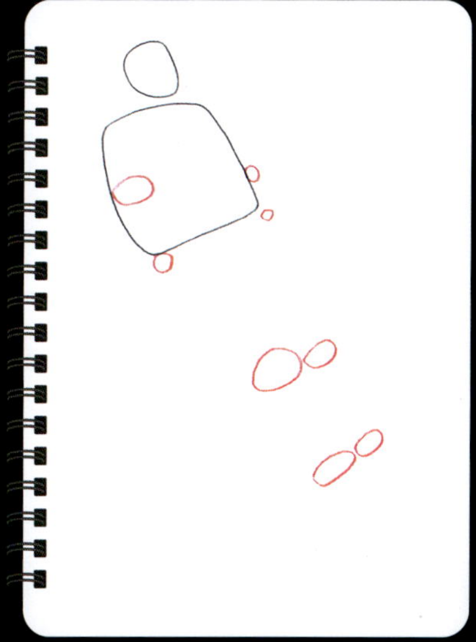

Step 3

Draw the neck, arms, legs, hands, and feet using the circles and ovals.

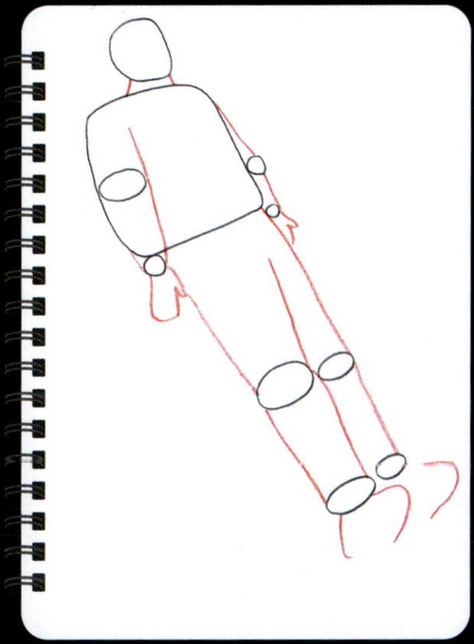

Step 4

Draw the outline of the lab table. Add the hairline. Add lines for the jacket and for the straps holding Frankenstein to the table.

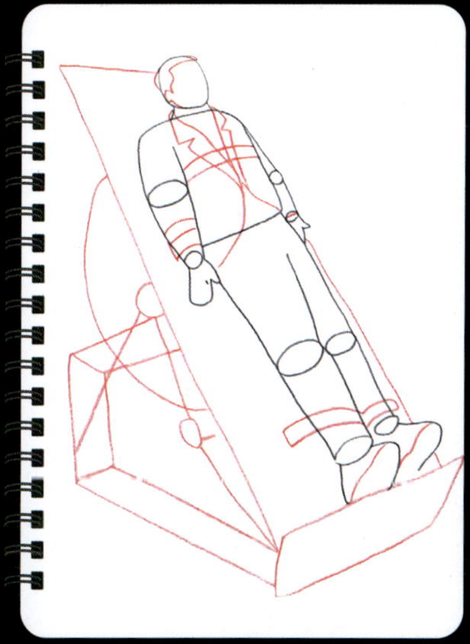

Step 5

Add details to the lab table and to the straps. Add the eyes, eyebrows, nose, and lips.

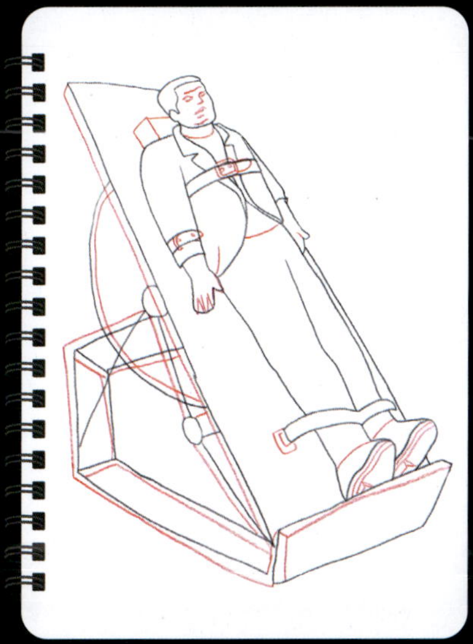

Step 6

Add details to the face and clothes. Now, color your drawing. Good job!

DID YOU KNOW?

Boris Karloff's costume for the 1931 movie weighed 48 pounds (22 kg)!

The 1960s television show *The Munsters* was a comedy about a family of monsters. The father, Herman, looked just like Frankenstein.

The name Frankenstein comes from a real place—a castle in Germany called Frankenstein Castle.

Mary Shelley was only 19 when she wrote *Frankenstein*.

Shelley's novel *Frankenstein* was written as part of a contest among friends to see who could write the best horror story.

Frankenstein is often green in films, but not in the book.

GLOSSARY

adaptations (ad-ap-TAY-shuhnz) Changing something from one form to another.

curse (KERS) A cause of unhappiness or harm.

evil (EE-vil) Bad.

icon (EYE-kahn) Something that is widely admired for having influence.

inspired (in-SPY-erd) To have moved someone to do something.

reputation (reh-pyoo-TAY-shun) The ideas people have about another person, an animal, or an object.

restore (rih-STOR) To put back, to return to an earlier state.

sequel (SEE-kwuhl) A book or movie that continues the story of an earlier work.

versions (VER-zhunz) Things that are different from something else, or having different forms.

violent (VY-lent) Strong, rough force.

INDEX

ON THE INTERNET

Frankenstein (Short Kids Version)

https://ririro.com/kids-books/frankenstein/

Read a short, kid-friendly version of Mary Shelley's *Frankenstein*.

Mary Wollstonecraft Shelley

https://kids.britannica.com/students/article/Mary-Wollstonecraft-Shelley/336363

Read more about the life of Frankenstein's author Mary Shelley with Britannica Kids. Explore more from the genre of gothic fiction, too.

Publisher's note to educators and parents: Our editors have carefully reviewed these websites to ensure that they are suitable for students. Many websites change frequently, however, and we cannot guarantee that a site's future contents will continue to meet our high standards of quality and educational value. Be advised that students should be closely supervised whenever they access the internet.